What Kind of Fruit Does God Like?

by J. Cecil Anderson

MW00509578

Written, illustrated and designed by J. Cecil Anderson

What Kind of Fruit Does God Like?
ISBN 978-0-615-27752-3

Scripture quotation is taken from the *Holy Bible* (King James Version).

P.O. Box 954
Fairburn, Georgia 30213

Manufactured in the U.S.A.

Dedication

To Father God for preparing me for such a great first book.
Thank you for your patience and blessings.

To my best friend, who is my wife, and our wonderful children.

To all who shared God's awesome Word with me as a child,
and to all the children Father God has privileged me to share with over the years.

Acknowledgments

A special thanks to all who contributed to the creation of this book.
May God richly bless you all.

I love to eat fresh fruit.
I eat some every day.

It helps me to grow strong.
That is what my mom would say.

It comes from Father God,
so in prayer my head I bow.

If you listen closely,
I will gladly teach you how.

Thank you God for this fruit.
You made it good to eat.
You gave for one, and for all,
this yummy, healthy, treat.

I am truly, very grateful,
and thanks I will always say.
I will remember, and not forget,
in Jesus' name I pray.

Now it is time to share and eat,
with Maria, Sarah, and Mike.

But, I often wonder,
and sometimes think,
what kind of fruit does God like?

Maybe He **loves** sweet, crunchy apples,
or do grapes bring Him **joy**?

Does He smile like I smile
when I get my favorite toy?

Is it peaches eaten in **peace**,
or pineapples that help me **wait**?

10

Is He happy like I am happy

when Dad fills my plate?

11

Oh, there are so
many fruits to choose,
and favorites for every tike.

Yet, I often wonder, and sometimes think,
what kind of fruit does God like?

It could be ripe, yellow bananas
I **gently** peel to bite.

Or is it cherries that taste so **good** and make every birthday just right?

16

Perhaps He likes sweet, juicy oranges,
as I like and **faithfully** seek.

Or is it the flavor of a pear,
that is as soft as I am **meek**?

Could it be delicious strawberries?
With these I need **self-control**.

It is really hard to eat just one.
They are much better by the bowl.

Oh, wait! I remember:
Galatians Chapter 5 verses 22 and 23.

That is where I find the answer.
Just take a look and see!

Galatians 5:22,23

But the fruit of the Spirit is love, joy, peace,
longsuffering, gentleness, goodness, faith, meekness,
temperance: against such there is no law.

See You Later!

The Fruit God Likes

Father God likes <u>all</u> kinds of fruit! He made it good, healthy and fun to share. Once, the Apostle Paul wrote a letter to the Galatians. In his letter he explained how Christians should act and he used fruit as an example. The way someone acts is called *character*. The character of Christians should always be kind and caring towards everyone they meet. This pleases Father God and is known as the **fruit of the spirit**.

 Love - to delight in or have real affection for others, even if they are unkind

 Joy - this is calm delight or a glad smile on the inside, even when things may not be going well

 Peace - to be relaxed and free from disturbance because Father God cares and He is in control

 **Longsuffering** (patience) - to wait for a long time; tolerant; slow to get upset or angry

 Gentleness (kindness) - to be nice, understanding and helpful to others, even when it is not easy

 Goodness - this means caring and doing good for others, just like Jesus did

 Faith (faithfulness) - to be trustworthy, reliable and dependable all the time

 Meekness - this means willing to listen, to learn and to put others first

 Temperance (self-control) - to control what we say and do, with the help of Holy Spirit

Nutritional and Fruity Facts

Apples - a good source of fiber and vitamin C; helps our bodies with digestion and helps us feel full after eating a meal

Grapes - provides vitamin C; helps to protect the cells in our body

Peaches - a good source of vitamin C; helps strengthen our immune system

Pineapples - an excellent source of vitamin C; helps our digestive system

Bananas - a good source of potassium and vitamin B; gives us extra energy, prevents cramps and helps our skin look healthy

Cherries - a good source of vitamin A, vitamin C and potassium; helps prevent tooth decay

Oranges - one orange contains all the vitamin C our body needs for a day; helps strengthen our immune system

Pears- a good source of fiber; helps our bodies with digestion

Strawberries - high in vitamin C; helps our heart stay healthy

Empowering generations... for greatness.™

CPSIA information can be obtained
at www.ICGtesting.com
Printed in the USA
LVHW080248040423
743411LV00002B/22